MOOD SWINGS

MOOD SWINGS

"Real Issues In Life"

TONETTE C. ROBINSON

authorHOUSE®

AuthorHouse™ LLC
1663 Liberty Drive
Bloomington, IN 47403
www.authorhouse.com
Phone: 1-800-839-8640

Published by AuthorHouse   10/22/2013

ISBN: 978-1-4918-3036-9 (sc)
ISBN: 978-1-4918-3011-6 (hc)
ISBN: 978-1-4918-3035-2 (e)

Library of Congress Control Number: 2013919112

Any people depicted in stock imagery provided by Thinkstock are models, and such images are being used for illustrative purposes only.
Certain stock imagery © Thinkstock.

This book is printed on acid-free paper.

CONTENTS

ACKNOWLEDGEMENT . . .

" *I'm giving thanks to my mother, Letha Ann Cheeks and father, Napoleon Robert Carey for dealing with my mood swings because they were a positive influence in my life over the years. It was not difficult for me to achieve goals when I became successful in anything I chose to pursue but their love always helped me along the way. When offering myself sincere advice, support encouragement and understanding real issues in life that I had to face in my unique, adult life, they showed me the light at the end of the tunnel. "You see, my parents always said that the choices I make in life are mine to decide upon and then, I could stand on my own two feet, not being defeated by anyone." "I am very thankful for their kindness and generosity in the times I had to face trouble, overcame it, and finally won the battle."*

"For the both of my children, Alexis C. Vick & Carl X. Robinson I am absolutely infatuated by their strong, awesome, love and support. My oldest; responsible, calm and caring daughter, Alexis is always there to assist everyone with whatever is necessary to get the task at hand completed. A very special thank you goes to my youngest; dear son, Carl, who is a superb, take charge individual with valuable insights on different issues is tops, I can complete this piece of literature on my own. My children give me reasons for living and have always been the backbone of my life since the beginning of conception. Our relationship together is an important one, both prestigious and respectful. I will never leave their sides especially whenever there is a problematic or unusual situation that tends to rise to the surface. We always work out our problems together producing a happy outcome for all of us involved. Lord knows, pleasant mood swings are felt throughout all the days of our lives but there are some days that are better than others. Every day though, is a time of loving each other, all the merrier. No matter what our faults may be, the end result is we always stick together through the great or hard times and it creates a bond that is untouchable. With the love of Jesus Christ by my side, I

am sympathetic, ecstatic and empathetic all together that our close relationship will last a lifetime."

"A shout out goes to all of the wonderful, marvelous people living in today's world! My real intentions are to lift you up, especially for those people experiencing a simple or complicated mood swing, that they may find it difficult to overcome it. For the people that are doing exceptionally well with whatever is necessary to be happy and successful, you are an excellent example for the rest of us thus, enjoying everything that life has to offer you."

"With the love of God, we can all survive mood swings when they develop as it only makes us stronger to deal with the real issue that we must face in life on an internal and external basis, but it takes inner strength, tenacity and optimism, to pull you through the mood swing and survive it in. It is heartfelt, that you will gain momentum and achieve success whenever you encounter a mood swing on your journeys because this piece of literature is presented to you with sincere knowledge. It will serve as a reminder of a tutelage of reflective information that you can use as a resource in everyday walks of life."

"It brings me with great pleasure to dedicate this piece of literature to all of the mood swinger's around the world with real issues in life they face and to my knowledge have made proper decisions. Life in general is pleasant for the person with the mood swing. They have found solutions to their internal/external problems thus, moving on with feeling better about themselves. Everything that goes along with it will allow them to continue to accomplish more goals which will help them in the short or long run, reach a milestone in their present personal or professional lives!"

SYNOPSIS . . .

" The contents of *Mood Swings, "Real Issues In Life,"* explains how people in society can possibly deal with their own mood swings felt throughout their lifetimes. This piece of literature provides valuable information to some of the everyday problems that some citizens face in reality beyond their control. Facts are full of information gained by reading the knowledge on the subject matter expressed to you, assumed to be true. As we become familiar with all different kinds of mood swings involving real issues we encounter in our personal and professional lives, they have a tendency to develop at the cost of no one person's own faults. As these issues arise from out of nowhere, it is how you handle them in life that gets you over obstacles, so that your situation improves for the betterment of human mankind. We do not always know the implication of exactly how it tends to invade one's life but we hope that it will show only positive results. *Mood Swings, "Real Issues In Life,"* is intended for the person to be informed and inspired after reading the chapters that we encounter in our daily walks of life. This piece of literature's sole purpose is to give some insight, intuitive, knowledge after reading the information that it provides to many people around the world, so it will help them achieve successful results within the individual, family, friends and people living in today's world."

PREFACE . . .

" *A*mericans and people around the world have mood swings every day. A strong desire overwhelms you with eager feelings as you are filled with all kinds of emotions that tear through you. Mood swings can change from one minute to the next. They can last for days, weeks, even months at a time and years to come when you least expect it to happen. This piece of literature might have some of the answers that you seek to some of your everyday problems. By closer evaluation of your inner strengths and weaknesses, will you turn out far better or your worst in life? After reading *Mood Swings, "Real Issues In Life,"* will you allow it to lift you up or tear you down? Expecting the best outcome requires doing some serious soul searching. Perhaps, you will be able to gain a new perspective on life. It is heartfelt, when closing the chapters in this piece of literature, will you know the real truth behind yourself because only you have the answers to that question?"

THE BIBLE

(King James Version)

I beseech you therefore, brethren, by the mercies of God, that ye present your bodies a living sacrifice, holy, acceptable unto God, which is your reasonable service.

And be not conformed to this world: but be ye transformed by the renewing of your mind, that ye may prove what is that good, and acceptable, and perfect, will of God.

For I say, through the grace given unto me, to every man that is among you, not to think of himself more highly than he ought to think; but to think soberly, according as God hath dealt to every man the measure of faith.

Romans 12:1-3

CHAPTER 1
WHAT IS TRUE HAPPINESS?

*I*f you could search for anything in life what would it be? Everyone believe that the emphasis should be on money but there is something more important than that, myth of conception. Why, the reality of the matter leads me to believe that everyone is in search of true happiness besides money. Many people have found it in most areas of their life, but there are still a few minor numbers of people who have not found it yet. But, while you are searching deeply for answers, the truth can be found locked from within your inner self. First of all, you must act like you want it. Secondly, you must believe you will receive it. Third then, it will come to you naturally.

After all, a surge of energy captures your attention span on the rise, true happiness then becomes characterized by a wave of good luck which happens to follow you. Ideally, you become fortunate of good things to come your way. Now, let's view how luck has an effect on true happiness. Some people believe though, they are not lucky people. Are these people really experiencing true happiness, considering good luck is a part of the true happiness nature and the two correlate with one another? So there is no myth of conception that the perception of luck cannot be misconstrued in most situations. While you receive it like the stroke of a genius; at the same time, we don't always get what we want. Humans create luck everyday by the situations that they put themselves in. Fortunate situations rise to the surface at moment's notice. There is an enormous amount of true happiness when you have received some form of good luck with it. It can also be found locked into your sensory perception. Therefore, if you put yourself in good, positive, and successful situations then, good luck in your fulfillment for true happiness normally follows you. Perhaps, this is where you gain momentum from feeling true happiness in most areas of your life when good luck is supplied with it.

There are many treasures to gain from receiving good luck and true happiness together in a number of ways. On a positive note, the bigger of life's necessities include buying a home and purchasing a new car. You are overwhelmed with joy as the salesperson has informed yourself that you are now the recipient of it. Perhaps, the boss has offered you that big promotion. You have risen to the top ladder of job success and it means more money for your family. These assets will make you endure true happiness throughout a life time. The dedication of achieving success, not failure is a set foundation towards receiving true happiness in both your personal and professional lives.

On the other hand, if there is failure then, a negative point to consider is to never become dismayed if things do not turn out as you had hoped for. By recognizing your own faults, you will focus on what impacts true happiness in most situations, and avoid negative occurrences to come in, and complicate your life. You will not allow negativity to spoil the pure nature of true happiness thus, it is better to avoid wreak havoc in your own life situations. However, sometimes we cannot avoid it but we must do what we can to get the proper resolution. Instead, searching for a happy outcome produces better results. Did you know, it is the soul's true happiness on the inside that allows us to be free of most distractions on the outside? Primarily because the more you are soulfully happy, the less you pay attention to those negative situations and negative attitudes! Worries become less distracted and you end up in a position that has allowed true happiness to take complete control over your life and the final decision to remain totally happy is yours to be successful in it if you want to be.

Most situations require us to be happy but there are some people who have a tendency to worry that things will not turn out as they had hoped for. Recently, after searching the World Wide Web, there was a brief article (2005) that is related to true happiness and it's subtext states: *"Don't Worry, Be Happy," "is an excellent reminder to always seek happiness, but the song may not be realistic in every life situation. Worrying is a part of life and happiness is not something you can pull out of a hat. While others undoubtedly can play a role in your happiness, ultimately it is up to you to create it for yourself. Happiness is within reach when you recognize and apply universal ingredients . . ."*

As we look at the whole picture and see ourselves doing some serious soul searching, true happiness affects the entire world and all members of a class or group under consideration to make a difference in the world in which we live. While we as citizens in society do not know each present or future implication, we realize what people should do to allow their inner strengths; desires and emotions help gain the best of their personality, traits and behavioral characteristics. It is only then that their outside persona non grata will flourish.

In true happiness, we need to analyze what is making a disturbance formulate a reaction that causes us to feel stimulus as situations arise from out of nowhere. We need to be strong enough to handle them by making ourselves improve a major impact that causes us to form an opinion about the disturbing reaction from certain areas of our lives. For example, if you allow someone to put you in a bad mood swing, seek resolution. The best way to handle it is think to yourself how you could rectify the situation. What can you do to turn the situation around in your favor? When we take proper precautions, we become extremely mindful of our circumstances. Therefore, we end up in a position that does not allow someone else to spoil the moment because it's a time with all due respect, we as individuals tend to shine by solving the situation.

As I read author, *Marci Shimoff's* piece of literature entitled: *"Happy for no Reason, 7 Steps to Being Happy from the Inside Out."* On page 5 in an excerpt she writes: *"My Hearts Request," This book was born of my deep longing to be happy. The kind of happy that is solid, true and anchored in my being, so that no matter what my external circumstances are, there is still a feeling of unshakable fulfillment, joy and inner peace. Other people lived this way, so I knew that it was possible. Yet, for so many years, no matter what I did, it seemed to elude me . . ."*

True happiness makes us in complete accord with each other where there are harmonious relationships with another relative, friend or person you meet in society. Over and over again, we need to build on our attributes together in order to sustain the relationship by allowing it to be true in our emotional well-being. The way to do this is to always be receptive and always ready for reconciliation whenever there is an disagreement. An example of this is relationships you encounter with people in society. Primarily, someone may walk up to you and greet you in some capacity. Your first impression was to ignore them because you may not have felt like speaking to him or her. Due to the nice way the other person spoke, you suddenly realize you were wrong and feeling a negative attitude. You wonder if somebody else would feel the same but they do not. Suddenly, due to the other person's disposition you realize that there was no harm in speaking them in the first place. As it turns out, they in return are not in the same mood you were in when you approached them. They felt better about themselves to speak back to you. The end result is that it is nice to know that there is someone out there who can brighten up your day. You then say, I will be the nicer individual and speak when I am approached by them and other people from now on. Therefore, if you relate to that person in a positive way, it will cause for a happy exchange of communication to transpire and it does not hurt anyone feelings in the encounter. In this scenario, people become harmoniously in sync with one another and have found a deep longing to maintain the true happiness mood swing in their relationships that will outweigh the negative feelings felt when one person approaches another person.

Let's also say that you are walking then, suddenly you have to wait at a stoplight, and a person stops next to you letting you know how bad their day is going. By falling deep into that negative feel may bring both of your days down. If you react to them positively with a true happiness frame of mind set then, the complete opposite reaction would occur in most situations. Not only would you maintain the positive and happy energy that you possess, but you may also show the other person that you encountered on your journey, that no matter how bad their day is going, it can always lead to true happiness down the road and a better outcome for the both of you when you lift each other's spirit up. In this picture, we build on positive and secure relationships and true happiness will also survive the negative vibrations the person whom encountered it seemed to be experiencing on that day.

In our daily lives, when we are faced with trials and tribulations, have you ever sensed that religion is beneficial to seeking true happiness? While there is no secret, we do find truth in our connection of our belief and faith as Christians believers in Jesus Christ's teachings of religion. As spiritual growth increases our belief in faith, we desire to live as true citizens of society facing a humbly life but we cannot always refrain from the abstract. When our society has put an emphasis on our physical well-being, leaning more toward spiritual growth in religious practices makes us true believers that we will endure true happiness as our lives are impacted spiritually. We become more satisfied with the status quo. All of our ways of survival needs have been met and everything we desire will be handed to us right at the door. We are happy people because receiving assurance will mean that it will be given to us through our faith in receiving true happiness. In many facets of life, when we pray at night, and ask for true happiness, we should not be afraid to live like we believe it in our daily lives as this is another way of how we overcome our trials and tribulations in a quest of endurance. Down the road, it is a tool that is always helpful after we have received our gift and/or rewards because Jesus Christ answers our prayers. We become more satisfied because our beliefs support us and it is beneficial to finding both faith and true happiness altogether when we have overcome our trials and tribulations. We will prosper by receiving a blessing from Jesus Christ and it calls for true happiness.

In the old testament of the book of *Ecclesiastes* chapter 2, verse 6 states: *"For God giveth to a man that is good in sight, wisdom, and knowledge, and joy: but to the sinner he giveth travail* [tribulation or agony; anguish] *to gather to him that is good before God, this also is vanity and vexation* [annoyance] *of spirit."* It relates to true happiness because the scripture says *"God giveth to a man that is good in sight, wisdom and knowledge and joy."* If he is a good person wouldn't that make his good behavior endure true happiness in his life. Perhaps, he has received a reward from God being blessed with money. We all know that generally, Jesus Christ blesses those who are good in life and makes a person feel true happiness. Now, if he was committing wrongful acts of sin, it is the way that we as inhumane citizens might encounter travail. As a result it may lead, down the road to critical times. However, most citizens choose to live a good life resulting in good behavior because Jesus Christ rewards us as good fellow American citizens here in the United States and from other countries. We are overwhelmed with joy as any gift we receive from God is a blessing resulting in true happiness instead of sadness and despair so that we are known in society to be instead, a great human being.

As I read Author, *"Amy Spencer's"* piece of literature: *"On the Bright Side up, 100 Ways to be Happy Right Now."* says on page 22 about the joy of good news that in my opinion results in feeling a sign of true happiness: *"But if you challenge yourself to find the good news about an ungood thing, you might find yourself laughing your way out. Use your imagination: start with the practical and go to the preposterous. Just say, the good news is . . . and like a game of Boggle where the person finds the most words among the letters wins, the more good news you can come up with about your situation the more you win."*

True happiness makes us feel victorious in situations beyond our control because it produces an extremely happy outcome. If you have done something positive to improve the impact of a lost situation, it results in solving the dilemma where true happiness about an ungood thing can actually turn into a positive solution for those people involved in whatever the problem appeared to be at the time. We will become truly ecstatic in some way, shape fashion or form that we have successfully triumphed over the turn of events and gotten positive feedback that pleases us. When a person institutes true happiness by eliminating negative thoughts in their mind or avoid slipping in a bad situation, positive feelings and attitudes will prevail all over you. You find yourself with the ability to challenge your way out of a negative situation and be truly happy that a good, positive reinforcement reaction from any un good circumstance has actually flourished. You are the one who received positive response that resulted in a major win for you. As a result, true happiness is a good thing and is felt from the inside and out.

We can exercise true happiness by avoiding improperly mistaking another person for their kindness geared towards us. There is only one kind of true happiness that is found from within the individual personal lifestyle. Only that person can see what they truly desire as individuals in a one-on-one encounter or group setting. We must realize that we should avoid stepping on someone else's toes too, as that only creates bad intentions for the people in question. What you should do is treat others the way you want to be treated. Then, you will receive the same kind of treatment in an exchange of good will feelings among you and no one becomes upset, hurt or angry.

In true happiness, set goals for yourself because by enacting the ability to put all your positive energy into what you can master will help you accomplish whatever you want out of life. We are realistic people and know that we can have whatever we choose to strive for in our society. This happens when we express positive feelings and emotions and go after what we truly desire in life. Then, a person will have reached his peak thus, receiving a plateau of success.

While the importance of true happiness is placed in a category all by itself, it has a high mark of value that can never be replaced primarily because the meaning of true happiness, is not something that should ever be taken lightly. When we act out our personal disposition, it also impacts that we have something powerful and meaningful to fulfill and enjoy in everyday walks of life. Then, we as people in society tend to stand out from a crowd expressing what our true happiness feelings really mean to us personally. We should always be ready show case our real talents creating a bond in our lives that is unbreakable. True happiness is within reach if you seek it. It is also safe to say that true happiness should never ever be taken for granted because the perception of it means exploring one's total inner and outer self.

With all the passion, excitement and ecstasy that people enjoy throughout their lives, if we embrace true happiness in all our life situations we as citizens will never lose sight of the path way that leads us to an endless world of opportunities. If we can accomplish every goal we try our hardest to achieve success in our quest. Then, true happiness for its fulfillment is just around the corner. We view it as a stepping stone to accomplishing many more goals that keeps us constantly receiving true happiness in the process.

CHAPTER 2
DEALING WITH GRIEF?

*A*re you at a point in your life when a period of grief has transpired at this time, from an occurrence not caused by your own self? You think to yourself what in the world has happened to you because all of a sudden you have suffered the loss of a loved one? In most situations, this will suddenly turn your world upside down. Why? Mainly because grief knocks on your door and makes you realize the reality that you will never acknowledge that person again in this life. True happiness has faded away for you at this time. Thus, depending on that relationship between you and your lost other one, you may lose not only that persons soul in nature, but it can also affect what you had going on with anyone physically, financially, emotionally and socially. For example, what if you lost a person whom you shared your only source of income (take for instance; a spouse or roommate) and you had to take care of the bills all by yourself? What would you do in this case? Perhaps, cutting back on expenses or seeking a financial planner would be helpful for the one who has to carry the weight right now. What if your lost one person and yourself were stressed out over a problem you are trying to solve and never quite got the answer to your dilemma? Who would be there to offer their insight to the both of you? Be careful though, pressures might create a mental block that could mount up at this time due to unpredicted situations going on beyond your control. When talking to another person who knows about the loss of your significant other one, that person could provide some feedback into the problem and help you solve your dilemma. What if you never got to tell the lost other one that you loved them and you expect the other person to love you back? How would you move on with your life? Would searching for another soul mate put all of your expectations back in a happy frame of mind turning the tables around for you? In most cases, my belief is that it could happen because beginning a new relationship is one way to overcome your previous losses with a former relationship. When these issues have positive results, grief could resolve itself at this time. However, at the time these events unfolded, you were probably wondering though, how did you put yourself in a position to be let down? You did not expect for it to happen to you but you encountered some minor disappointments along the way. What you are probably experiencing right now is something that puts you in a deteriorating fad of a mood swing. The mood swing that passes through you is what can be called a period of dealing with grief. Grief is defined as a deep, mental, anguish, emotion stemming from bereavement of some kind of a situation. While all of the issues mentioned above can cause grief in your past or present lifestyle, how do you deal with it? Be extremely careful that it does not lead into future complications. Could it be, you may or may not have been totally responsible for what turned into a disaster so it results in harm to you because you are going through some periods of dissolution from your present or past circumstances? You are holding on to regrets in your body, mind, soul, spirit and heart because you have become annoyed at the mood of frustration when it increases in a mental and emotional capacity.

In order to handle it, we often see it difficult to pick up the pieces from where you last felt the problem but you must be willing to tackle the problem. In reality, you need strength, endurance and a strong mind to abstain from the mental block. There must be a dire need to explore and weigh your options thus; solving what can be done to improve the impact of a depressing situation. By coming to grips with the nature of the problem gets you over obstacles that are in the way. Grief will not lead into future complications if you move to resolve the negative vibrations you feel at a point in your life when you are holding on to it for long periods of time. It is not recommended though, that you sit in isolation, either. You are not in an emotional position that you should be your own problem solver but also talk out the situation causing the annoyance with someone else so they can be of help. Simply say, I have a problem I need to address or can you help me with this problem and you just might be surprised at the outcome.

It is of vital importance not to live in the past. Do not hold on to past and present regrets as grief has a tendency to set back your personal life's goals and potential accomplishments. Now, it is inevitable that grief will temporarily block reality due to the nature of remembering and reflecting back on past and/or current memories of a lost situation. It is also important that you do not over react on moments when you think you should be, could be, or would be acting out on a lost love one's life, personalities, and actions so it is a good rule of thumb to avoid getting too emotionally involved with the lost person's life in question. Rather reflect on the positives of life lessons learned that your lost loved one used to bring to the table when they were alive. By doing so, you interact their vision with yours by acting on these philosophies positively of being the stronger person to overcome the grief-stricken phase that you are dealing with at that time. By nature, you have made better progress in your life and a wise decision to abstain from the grieving process but to move on with living your life in better times by your own choice.

There was an author by the name of *James Van Praagh*, he wrote this piece of literature: *"Healing Grief, Reclaiming Life After Any Loss." "Why is there grief and why do we have to go through it? Grief serves an important purpose. It is a reaction to our loss. It represents our underlying sense of insecurity. Our fears of abandonment and feelings of vulnerability rise to the surface, forcing us to face them. The world upon which we predicted our belief systems, goals and our lives in general is suddenly out of control. We feel scared and exposed. Most of us don't want to deal with or feel these negative emotions and yet, they are just relevant and as important to our well-being as our positive feelings."*

From a psychological point of view, while on a routine basis, change your thinking habits. Do not allow negative thoughts to linger in your mind for long periods of time. By doing so, we remove a burden of grief placed on our mind to turn into positive ways of seeking change. For example, during a period of sorrow, we should also avoid punishing ourselves for something that ultimately consumed our nature and made us feel down about different situations or circumstances out of control. Ask yourself, am I going to abstain from this period of annoyance? If you are willing to be the stronger person then, the answer is probably, yes! You can make a wise choice to refrain from this nuisance by causing you an overwhelming response to admonish the grief hidden inside of your sensory perception and put it away from you forever.

Grief can interfere with and cause major complications in your life when all kinds of mishaps hamper your progress to get on with your life. An example of this would be when my family suffered the loss of my maternal grandmother recently. She was terminally ill suffering from a long, severe medical illness. All of the family, friends and associations were torn apart by the loss of this loved one because she was a very dear and close family member to us. At the funeral for her burial following the services, everyone was sobbing from her departure of this life. Family, friends and guest were feeling tremendous amounts of agony and grief. However, what actually calmed everyone down was the mere thought that everyone realized that my maternal grandmother were no longer suffering in this life. When the pastor read her obituary out loud, everyone knew that she had finally found peace within herself due to passing away from her illness. Then, grieving at this point started to turn a sad situation into a good, positive one and everyone realized the pain and suffering within herself had ceased. She would only be remembered in spirit. We came to this conclusion that it was heartfelt, among the entire attendees at the funeral service, that it is best not to mourn over the loss of a loved one but we should all be happy for her departure. She has gone to a different place and the Lord has called her home. In realistic terms, we got over her loss by reminiscing about the good times we shared with her when she was alive. At the same time, it is better to take everything positive that the deceased has taught us and make it better. My grandmother was always positive and spiritual, so she had infused that within us. I can now start to regain my sense of accepting that grief will not be the end of the world for me. Turning a negative situation into a positive one removes a slow period of burden placed on my mind that will go away in due time.

In the book of *Psalms*: chapter 31, verse 9 talks about grief. The verse reads: "*Have mercy upon me, O*

Lord for I am in trouble: mine eye is consumed with grief, yea, my soul and my belly."

Is it a pre-meditated circumstance where grief can come in and troubles make you feel at a point there is no way left to turn? There is a tendency that when it consumes your nature, it will make us sick if succumb to the likes of it. Questions of bereavement leave you asking yourself just what should you do about it? How will you actually overcome it? Who will be the number one person to talk to? Perhaps, receiving the spiritual guidance of your pastor at the church you attend, then, he or she would be more than welcome to assist you. Resources can be of help with places you can go to in a time of need. Be receptive and communicate positively to explain the problem, thoroughly. It is pertinent that you do not lose focus your insight but that you remain in reality. Never give up where your paths lead you but looking up to God, he will have mercy on your soul.

We as citizens need to recognize that to deal with grief may mean making a fresh start. Just say, it will not take control of my life and make me feel down about the situation exceeding beyond my maintaining self-control. Instead, decide what is best for me to work out my problem. For example, make a responsible decision to get away from the period of annoyance. A good rule of thumb is to tell yourself that we should hearken to heed our own thought processes. Then, the pathway ahead would be much clearer than you would imagine because there is something positive returns our sense of reality back into focus and to our normal state of mind. Then, we are no longer troubled about the impact of a negative mood swing that we happen to feel there was no way to pull us out of the situation. But, by finding an outlet to relieve the stress and burden, will get us over the pain and suffering of a mental and emotional distress to solve a problem nagging away at us.

Are you having trouble or difficulty making a positive change to move from old situations to new ones? It would not hinder your progress if changing your position gives you a whole new outlook on life. We need to move away from feelings of being wronged in society. Instead, channel your positive energy into moments of feeling totally good about yourself. At this time, the emphasis on grief is something that will be placed on the back burner because you have decided to rise above it. You have removed the burden of a mental block that is just sitting there to get on your nerves. A sadden, emotional frustration diminishes away because dealing with it on a positive level means you have decided to move on to the next phases of healing that part of life that made you feel down about a circumstantial evidence that is assumed to be true. For instance, the loss of a loved whom you know, realistically and emotionally that you can get over the pain and move on with your life. It requires restoring your life from this annoying period of grief reminiscing about the good times you shared with that someone. Talk to people that can be an ear to listen to so the situation will not take its toll on you. More importantly, always figure out that there is a way to control it. Realize, there are positive ways to get over hard times as dealing with grief in situations is where we will overcome it and after that we can move on with our lives.

Chapter 3
Overcoming Anxiety

There are times when an annoying situation you cannot surpass up from a particular or peculiar person in a domineering position, rises to the surface. A person comes along and pushes your buttons the wrong way. Rather than look the other way, you want to get even but you cannot at this time. You want to become confrontational due to wanting to get some pent-up frustrations out of your system. There becomes a period of isolation as you are pondering what next to do to this individual. You are feeling as if the other person is responsible for whatever caused the attack. When your feelings take recourse in this manner, anxiety comes in and is a state of uncertainty and, disturbance of the mind regarding uncertain events. It is the same as being apprehensive of intense, often disabling fear caused by the anticipation of something threatening like an eager or agitated desire by oneself to hang on to negative vibrations suffered by that person or an instinct situation. What is the underlying cause of this anxiety anticipation of a mood swing? How do you handle it? What should you do in order to get over an attack of anxiety made on you? In other words, how would you overcome it now? As we look at anxiety further, here are a number of other ways it actually builds up. Perhaps, you have found out that you and another person are brothers but your lack of knowing your father and having not been grown up around him creates anxiety for you. You wonder if your father will accept you or will he offer parental guidance for you all throughout your stages of childhood, adolescence and adulthood. What if you found out that your girlfriend is cheating on you with your best friend? Seemingly, the two of them together tears you apart. You are disappointed over the break up in the relationship but you have to pick up the pieces of where the relationship tore apart. However, you decide that it's not best for you to mend fences at this time instead, let it go. What would you do when a sister that is four years apart in age difference from yours, receives better treatment from your mother than yourself. Why is your mother always expressing an indifferent attitude towards you, and finding fault with almost everything that you do. The mother is always showing favoritism towards the other daughter that she likes the most. You think that the other person does not like you for some reason. You ask yourself what have you done to the family to receive this kind of treatment. One thing for sure, is you are probably thinking someone has hurt your feelings and a negative reaction against the other individual is on your mind due to feeling these periods of anxiety. You wonder why you are not liked by the people that you are supposed to be close with. You have not gotten even with the other person but all you can think about is the rage made against you for the vengeance you seek and this causes frustration. At this time, while anxiety increases in an emotional capacity, there is no need to punish the attack made on you. On the other hand, you could calm down and think, what is your other alternative? Are you going to overcome the anxiety mood swing you feel between you and the other person?

Anxiety is so intense it has tendency to upset you tremendously if you succumb to the likes of it. It is important not to allow pinned up feelings to get the best of you inside of your emotions mentally. It is important to disconnect from your instinctive nature when dealing with this issue. If you trust your instincts when dealing with an emotional problem like an attack of anxiety will become conflicting because of the negativity that is associated with the emotion of feeling as if someone does not like you. Instincts are natural human reactions just like breathing. If you compound that along with an unfortunate situation(s) that can occur like the ones mentioned above, then your instinct becomes clouded due to the hurt feelings that came along with it. Anxiety has a tendency to make a person worry that something disturbing is going to start to happen to that person feeling it. Anxiety could actually get on your nerves and complicate your life entirely from the wrong impact of the nature of the problem making it difficult for you to solve it.

"Muriel MacFarlaine," author of, *"The Panic Attack, Anxiety Phobia Solutions Handbook,"* says on page

15: *"An anxious person is apprehensive and continually feels worried, ruminates and anticipates that something unpleasant will happen. The individual feels, "on edge," impatient or irritable. This sound familiar because it is a human condition to be anxious some of the time but the question is: Where does "normal" anxiety end and "abnormal" anxiety begin? Where does mere concern change and become marked discomfort or extremely intense panic? The answer to that question is complex. Some of the answer lies in an understanding of how our nervous system works, how our personalities are formed, and how we view the world around us. And, what we do to respond to our nervous system's signals."*

Looking at overcoming anxiety from a physical standpoint but thinking about retaliating through the body is first on your mind. It is what the mind or spirit is telling you to act on but, this is not a good idea to do. By ignoring your inner thoughts, you avoid a physical confrontation. Mentally, the mind is a powerful weapon. With anxiety, there is a tendency to hold onto ill feelings inside of it that you have been made to feel less superior to the other individual. You should avoid bullying tactics to put you in a negative frame of mind made by the other individual. It only becomes more difficult to overcome your weaknesses. By being the stronger person than he or she is, you can conquer it. Emotionally, you are readily affected with stirred up emotions. Your thoughts are concentrated on seeking revenge, instead of the other person admitting have I done something to upset you? Find out what the underlying causes of the anxiety mood swing is between you and other person. The person causing the frustration might respond no, have I hurt your feelings? I am sorry for making you feel this way. I had no intention to do this to you. Will you forgive me? You are probably thinking it was an unusual circumstance that caused it and the determination to resolve any wrong communication makes the both of you feel more comfortable to make it right again.

Opening up and being receptive to the other person could solve a minor dispute between clashing people. The positive way to handle it is to try talking out your differences with the other person first, to see if you can discuss the issue with them openly. This allows for feedback from all parties involved. If the other person does not feel like talking then they just may walk away avoiding a response to you. They will come back when both sides are receptive enough to agree on subject matter. One of the things that will happen is a sudden sigh of relief when you decide to come to grips with an antagonizing pain that you feel from discussing this issue openly. Perhaps, you have thought this episode out realizing that there was a mistake in your pre-judgment of the assuming that one person does not like you. Deciding to mend broken fences by discussing the dispute openly is the only way to solve it. If your first reaction is to seek a reprimand for revenge, instead of solace until you can figure out how to solve the situation and cannot handle the pressure perhaps, seeking a counselor is recommended because someone may have made you have ill-feelings caused from a bundle of nerves that requires you to seek a physician for assistance.

Henry Emmons, M.D., wrote *"The Chemistry of Calm,"* and his piece of literature states on pages 5, 6: *"Fear, worry, stress and compulsivity, the unpleasant and unproductive states known collectively as anxiety, are even more common than depression. Anxiety states* are increasingly frequent, especially in recent times. Like depression, the effects of anxiety extend beyond the body and mind to the entire being, affecting not only one's sense of well-being but also health, longevity, work production, relationships-the entire human condition."

The World Wide Web states this subtext in (wikihow.com): "Without warning, your heart races, your stomach churns, you do not know what to do and troubles that look easy for other people to handle seem like their bringing down your entire world. You hold onto hope that you can keep your nerves calm, but you can't. You start to discover the things that set you off, but you can't avoid them all. And, there are always unexpected situations."

According to the World Wide Web, there was a section on *Understanding Anxiety (anxiety.com 2012)* states: *Anxiety affects 1 in 7 people in Australia, making it even more common than depression. The fact is everyone feels anxious from time to time. It's a normal and natural response when a person feels threatened or is worried that something bad or unpleasant might happen.*

We could have a reaction to the situation by negatively responding to the other person that we do not know how to communicate our feelings positively. We have a tendency to believe the opposite reaction to an otherwise easier method to solving disputes among clashing people is the first response. When this happens, it only enables more anxiety but, we need to explore other options to handling it, so encounters and situations we involve ourselves in turns out better than we have hoped. As much as we worry that the other person may not like one's self, it would be advisable to go to the source and find out what is necessary for change in our dealings with each other. Instead, this could result in positive attitudes towards coming to grips to resolve the whole issue that stirred up pent up emotions in the first place.

Anxiety can cause stress because you are constantly worried that someone is picking on you. It is not okay to feel this way. Your state of mind might deteriorate at this time. You may not come to the realization that it could be all in your mind. Can you turn away from stressful situations that may make your nerves frigid? Will you go to another person and talk out your differences, instead? It can happen if you are willing to put you them aside and gain a whole new perspective on life. Put your mind to it and say I will not let these negative feelings get the best of me. Be receptive and speaking to the other person with suggestions to improve the impact of the terrible situation. Simply say, I am sorry if I hurt you. If you decide not to apologize, it will only make you more determined to worry about a frustrated situation. A situation like acting if you cannot stand the other person, do your best to avoid more disappointment at this time. It is also not a bad idea to walk away from the attack made on you until you can address it at a later time. Then, that negativity won't cause you to hold on to it for long periods of time. Realistically, what you need to do is let go of lingering thoughts in your mind. It only makes you more upset. If it bothers you to the point of pondering issues that you cannot solve, then move to resolve the issue after you have thought it out thoroughly. At this point, you may realize that anxiety should not allow your mental well-being to suffer for a long period of time. You might experience that the other person wants to talk out the disagreement with you and resolve any angry, hurt feelings. Overcoming anxiety is a two-way step for a means to achieving an end. One side has to be willing to communicate with the other side. The other side should express a dire need to explain the situation to the one that is hurting thus; it only creates finding a resolution to reaching an understanding with the one who is feeling the anxiety attack on them. Making up only makes you both feel better about yourselves again. If both sides do not want to come to an agreement, it is recommended to wait until a later time that the other person feels like talking to you.

Getting over it requires finding a solution to resolve those negative impacted encounters that has taken a strain out of yourself. Consequently, it is a feeling that makes you think that someone does not like you. It is advisable to approach the person in question and see if they want to resolve the issue with you. Once a decision has been reached, you start to feel good about yourself again. It is at this time, you will know that your anxiety period can go away and the mood swing will result in making your relationship with each other turn out far better than you would imagine.

CHAPTER 4

THE CAUSES OF DEPRESSION

Some people have felt depression in our society for ages. It is considered to be an over powering force that is domineering if you allow it to control you. Depression causes your physical and mental emotions to suddenly take on an illness that may complicate your life if you are not careful. It stems from a condition of deep dejection characterized by a lack of response to stimulation and withdrawal from reality. At this time, you are feeling periods of sadness that is causing you to feel deeply low in spirits. There are questions that need to be addressed at this time. Have you ever been depressed? Why, are you feeling this way? What is putting you in a depressing state of mind? While you have difficulty trying to familiarize your imagination with reality, why do you withdraw from it? Could it be you feel that everything is going wrong for you? I bet you feel like there is no one to talk to or is it that you don't feel much like talking to the other person? What are other signs of depression? Are you going through a period of constant sadness? Do you have trouble sleeping or feeling irritability? Is there a feeling of hopelessness? Are you guilty of something for no reason? Are you low in energy, fatigued or feeling worthless and have you noticed a significant weight change in your health?

Staying in a positive active frame of mind helps eliminate depression. Do not try to kill yourself. When you become focused on living life in a fun and peaceful manner, those suicidal-like thoughts dissipate due to you not allowing yourself to think about it. Negative thoughts become negative actions once your thought processes have deteriorated about a pre-planned circumstance that you have dwelled into from an occurrence. Do something that has always been a fun pastime for you and involve others that you care about to join you. This will bring you into a calm state, thus allowing you to be free of anger, and surrounding yourself around peers that you care about to allow you to talk about any problem(s) that has kept you in a depressive state of mind. The reason for people contemplating suicide during depression is due to being too much in the negative now past and present, instead of looking towards the positive present and future. Regardless of how your life is going at that point, do you think that giving up your life's immortality is worth the immediate risk to end your life? Now you don't necessarily know where you will be in 1 year, 5 years, or even 10 years from now, but wherever you end up at, you should be doing whatever it takes to better yourself each day. Every human being has a problem from the wealthiest to the poorest, so does that mean that we should kill ourselves when we face a challenge that we seem to be unable to handle? It is in our nature to face challenging problems, and the thrill of life is the joy of concurring daily life problems and situations regardless of our physical, mental and social way of life and solving what complications arise to the surface. Also know that there is always somebody out here in the world that will listen. Some people are more difficult than others but there is always somebody to listen to your problems because again, "WE ALL HAVE SOME PROBLEMS AND SITUATIONS THAT OCCUR EVEN IN OUR NORMAL LIVES!"

A small article on the internet about symptoms of depression (*depression.com 2012*) states: *Do you have symptoms of clinical depression? Sure, most of us feel sad, lonely, or depressed at times. And, feeling depressed is a normal reaction to loss, life's struggles, or an injured self-esteem. But, when the feelings become overwhelming and last for long periods of time, they can keep you from leading a normal, active life.*

There are some critical things to notice when you feel like you are in a depressed state. It is to your advantage not to allow a problem to fester in your mind. Do not waste time and effort into negativity, but to keep your connection with reality in the present and future tense, no matter how painful it feels. If you allow problems to build up means, that they are still in the pit of your stomach, meaning that no matter how difficult the problem is, it is still an unresolved situation. Whatever the situation is, depression will continue to affect your psyche until it is lost and unresolved thoughts are no longer inside of you. The longer you allow it to hold you down, whatever the depressed situation is, the more it wastes time for you to move on to different and more positive facets of what life has to offer you. The more you haven't come to grips with reality of how you feel, the more you have disconnected yourself with reality, because of how you feel, and what you say about how you feel is like feeling a different recourse to the problem building up but in the realm of life you must face reality.

Author, *David M. Burns* writes on page 261 on his piece of literature: *"Feeling Good, The New Mood Therapy." "When your depression has vanished, it's a temptation to enjoy and relax. Certainly, you're entitled. Toward the end of therapy, many patients tell me they feel the best they've ever felt in their lives. It sometimes seem that the more hopeless and severe and intractable the depression seemed, the more extraordinary and delicious the taste of happiness and self-esteem, once it is over."*

Realistically, you must ask yourself why am I allowing whatever the depression may be, to get me down. There are situations like losing your job, being teased for no reason and you are under excruciating pressures from family problems. When something in society is often threatening may be reasons you feel this way. Again, you have to put yourself out of a negative frame of mind and seek an outlet to get you active in something that resolves all your worries.

The World Wide Web had this to say on: (Depression.com), *"What Causes Depression:"* *"Depression can be caused by a variety of factors. Since genetics play a role, if a family member has experienced symptoms of depression, you may be a higher risk of developing depression yourself. Major hardships and life stressors such as the death of a loved one or loss of a job, may also being about depression. Whatever the cause of depression, it's important to realize that it is a medical illness, just like diabetes or heart disease. It is not something that is your fault or a sign of weakness. It is a medical illness that needs to be treated."*

This statement was on the internet: (Depression. com), *"How Can I Tell If I Have Depression."* *"Everyone feels sad from time to time but these feelings usually pass rather quickly. In these situations, this is not depression. Depression feels different. Someone with depression experiences extreme sadness or despair that lasts more than a couple of days, extending to weeks and even months. People who are truly depressed find that symptoms can interfere with normal, everyday activities, such as going to school or work, even eating or sleeping. They often feel helpless and hopeless, like giving up."*

Depression has a tendency to make you sit around and ponder negative thoughts. You sit around and pout! You take deep breathes by sighing in and out. But, taking things slowly and one day at a time is an excellent remedy.

Do not constantly live in a world of depression. There is no reason for you to feel sadness or despair but it can happen to anyone. To our rescue, there is actually someone you can turn to. By seeking a medical professional can provide a way to treat the condition of depression. There are all kinds of information in pamphlets that explain what causes depression in some people. Social groups are always there to be of help, too. All of these resources will give you some insight, intuitive, knowledge into the subject matter helping you overcome what could be a serious problem by seeking treatment for the causes of depression. Chances improve for the betterment of human mankind. You will feel better for yourself in the long run and this could help you overcome the causes of depression and rid it from your life forever.

CHAPTER 5
WHEN EXCITEMENT
STRIKES AT YOU!

*W*hen excitement strikes at you, why do you feel this enormous sign of ecstacy? The truth of the matter is when it happens, you turn out truly ecstatic for some eventful situation or circumstance, and this excited mood swing is good for the soul, primarily because you are also feeling excellent in spirits, too. A person feeling excitement is never depressed and it has taken a back seat from feeling turned away from a world of excitement in reality. A cheerful attitude takes precedence over your imagination and allows you to overcome a down in the dump feeling by getting the most out of life. One of the things that can happen is it can put you in great company with other people. For example, excitement is something as simple as attending a baby shower and all of the guests are in a social gathering together pleasantly having a great time with one another. They are excited because they are exchanging gifts, eating cake thus, having a jolly ol' time. Winning an award is another form of excitement for the fact; you are thrilled at the mere satisfaction that you have received an accolade for your hard work and dedication to human mankind. These positive vibrations enhance a desire for you to enjoy these moments of excitement because as it strikes at you there is a positive response to feeling passion with the one thing that is causing you to release an ecstatic mood swing. Excitement always arouses a strong feeling in activities because you become excited in some capacity about whatever you are involved in. Adrenalin rushes to your brain almost every time and stirs up emotions that become strong in nature. In general, we all get excited about something but there are some people that feel it more than others. The people that do have an overwhelming desire to be the life of the party and it is the same as being the recipient of a surprise party planned out for you, winning the lottery, or receiving a dream vacation. This is primarily because excitement can strike at you like a blow to the head.

Excitement can be a breakthrough and change in your life. I think a great example is if you got your career job. I would be more excited if I got a raise after a big project completed rather than getting praise that everybody normally gets at work. You know that you can start planning things ahead for your future. It is also important that you use excitement striking at you as a momentum swing to change and alter other things in your life. It could even be something as realistic as seeing a friend that you haven't seen in 10 years, and they are moving on the same block as you. Whenever excitement strikes at you, embrace it, enjoy it, and let it make you and/or your family/friends/peers look at life in a positive way. Generally, the higher the excitement, the bigger the accomplishment will turn out to be.

From a phychological point of view, it is the mind's emotional responses that let you know you are excited in some capacity. I would simply say that excitement has positive reactions when you become it and it becomes you. For example, you become more like an hour glass that is full as the particles of time pass away on the clock. But, it tends to make you think are you a happy individual or a disappointed with my mistakes, kind of thinker. If you decide to look at it another way instead of the "bad news you accept good news first. You become a "good news or great news" kind of thinker. Being excited means to me, "no matter what obstacles are being thrown my way, I am figuring out how to handle and accomplish goals, and not taking "<u>No</u>!" for an answer." You are solutions oriented when you are excited, and procrastination is never an option. The hard part is those situations where only negativity surrounds you, chances are you won't take negativity for an answer and your surrounded peers won't take positivity for an answer away from you.

"Ian K. Smith, M.D.", wrote a piece of literature, *"Happy, Simple Steps to Getting the Most out of Life."* On page 183 of his excerpt states: *"Why do acts of kindness work? Many believe that they bolster one's self-regard, increase the number of positive social interactions, and enhance charitable feelings toward others-all things previously believed to make people*

happier. Acts of kindness can inspire others to like you more and have a greater appreciation of your behaviors, and potentially they can lead to reciprocal kindness. One of your basic human needs is to feel connected to someone else and establish some type of meaningful relationship. Committing acts of kindness satisfies this need. Excitement is simple as expressing it throughout your dealings with other people that cause for pleasant exchanges of gratitude. It could be offering a tip to a waiter in a restaurant by thanking themselves for extending a helpful hand to you in a time of need. When meeting someone for the first time by walking pass them on the street and speaking to that person exudes real acts of kindness. You are happy to greet each other. A person whom you became friends with that you met for the first time also brings back excitement to you. The point being made here is that in these three scenarios you are real excited to approach someone with a one on one encounter with each other. It is because excitement puts you in a positive active, frame of mind. Once it opens up your spirit becomes extremely lively to meet these encounter and exchange positive connections. You are full of life, energy and vigor. Gaiety and an animated intelligence liven up your body, mind, soul and spirit. Ideally, you are the one effervescent and a sparkling individual to approach/be approached by someone with an extremely high spirited personality being kind to you, the same way you were kind to them. It will make the both of you excited people. Do not confuse excitement with being in the comfort zone primarily because someone could mistake you for your kindness. It is pleasing to know that someone has a friendlier attitude and you become excited that someone has actually offered an act of kindness to you but we should not allow someone to take advantage of our kind, excited spirited nature. If meeting an encounter you are not generally receiving positive feedback and someone is only out for gain. Greed could one of the reasons you end up with hurt feelings. The person is pretending to be a friend when they are not. The best thing to do is remove yourself away from them so you do get hurt in the process. You can restore the excited mood swing by becoming a participant with some other connection and meeting some person/situation or circumstance that does not take advantage of you to approach them in a kind, excited manner. How the situation is handled by you is by searching for a better outcome that is a true sign of what makes a person excited about being pleased of the turn out because you have accomplished the goal.

The World Wide Web *(excitement.com)* has this approach to most situations: *"You don't always have to hyper and crazy! Simply, talk more and dance around and hug people. Do things that nobody would expect and standout. Be a weirdo!"* It also means *hang with the right crowd. If you have friends (co-workers as the case may be) that are known to be a stick in the mud (boring) harsh or crude (bad reputations), don't let them make your life dull. Some people are just so out there and crazy that others look at them as a bright and exciting people. The question posed to you is, do you want to be more interesting or thrilling? How do you keep excitement in a relationship? What do you do when you feel like you are in a rut with your significant other? You renew the spice and don't be afraid to unlock the passion you have buried. You will both laugh or engage in intimacy!"*

Excitement is expressed where two people tie the knot for the first time. Both the bride and groom have received assurance that the wedding is definitely going to take place. The wedding date is even being moved up because they cannot wait to become a married couple. After they wed, there are no mixed feelings between them because the marriage was definitely an excited, momentous occasion. The couple realizes that love may last for the rest of their lives. Though, there could be a circumstance where the marriage may have some minor disagreements somewhere down the road. However, the two of them are able fix any problems. The couple is so excited that there is marital bliss between them outweighing any problems that tend to arise on occasion tends to resolve itself. Keeping the marriage strong is what makes it excited to last throughout a lifetime.

When excitement strikes at you, you should go all out to accomplish your goal. Be a people pleaser that definitely overcomes obstacles that are in the way. Do not get yourself tangled up in negative situations allowing it to put you in a negative mood swing. In most situations, do not be the one who constantly gets upset or angry with your past, present or future circumstances. You are not allowing someone else to bring your world down emotionally. When excitement strikes at you as a person, the more ecstatic you are as an individual when the more you become it, it will grab a hold of you in a major way.

Chapter 6
Are You A Shameful Person?

*H*as a feeling of shamefulness started to take precedence by yourself as an individual, or an instinctive situation? Suddenly, has a tendency to make you to feel let down when something embarrassing happens has transpired? What have you done that has caused you a negative feeling that is disgraceful leaving a poor image of one's self and this is from an miserable attack made from yourself. Thus, you are shameful of the mood because of something misleading happening within your realm? An example of it is feeling embarrassment from an indecent proposal. It is unseemly offensive to have good reactions at this time, because another person has propositioned you with a request that you cannot accept, and that puts you in an immodest frame of mind. Why do you to feel these moments of shamefulness? Would you change your position and decrease your level of shyness, and being timid, in nature? The answer is probably, no because at this time your first feelings is to withdraw from the sudden distraction. However, some people feel this way, others do not feel it. Do you feel outside of your comfort zone? Have you hidden yourself from the world? You might in some situations where the circumstance actually occurred at this time. I think in most shameful situations, you have put yourself in an out of the ordinary reaction to stimulus. It is an agent or action or condition that elicits or accelerates a physiological or psychological activity or response about human nature. It is also something that excites or arouses a reason for people to respond to actions of a person's emotional well-being and shy away from the situation that has occurred suddenly if you are having a reaction to it.

What you need to do is try, and separate, and acknowledge shamefulness and disappointment. A great example is any form of work abuse. Most people spend a majority of their day at the workplace. If there is a situation that occurs where a male or female co-worker is assaulting you mentally, physically or emotionally, you should find somebody to communicate to like another staff member. Management is also advisable with another supervisor or manager. More importantly, remember that you were the victim and not the abuser. You shouldn't feel the need to be negative towards yourself for that situation to occur. The fact that someone feels like they can take advantage of you in that environment is shameful on them, and you should not be disappointed at yourself. This is a mood swing that leads down to a road of negativity and self-doubt. You are generally disappointed at the status quo. Some people respond to it, others tend to not let it bother them. Now, in some situations when you feel like you are ashamed of yourself, it is important to remember that you probably did not give it your all and that whatever situation(s) occurs again, you remember your previous shameful experience so that you know you do not want to repeat it again. Thus, you move towards achieving respect because you are more comfortable in a new surrounding as you did not know you would encounter a negative episode of feeling a period of shamefulness.

There could even be a reaction to shamefulness causing you to have a bundle of nerves, when you are approached with a pre-meditated circumstance, to tackle the situation head on. There are nervous intentions and bad vibrations to it. Your reaction puts you in a negative frame of mind because of being scared that you have done something wrong will be your first reaction. It is the same as being yelled at for doing something totally unappreciated and/or unpredicted that you thought it was okay to do. You shake and quiver and feel shameful that you are in fact, embarrassed about the scene. It causes you to turn away from being the very best that you can be in life but by being extremely mindful of the negative impact you encounter then, you won't lose your lack of accomplishing goals. As you seek a willingness to overcome it does not become you and you do not become it. Being shameful is being afraid to deal with your past or current occurrences. You might carry the situation with you too far and as long you can hold on to the problem. An example would be if you spill an order of food on you, or you have to ask the waiter if you can be excused from the table. If you are afraid to talk it out may have you feeling a sign of embarrassment and it makes you want to withdraw from the incident in question. Be careful, not to allow shamefulness to drive you to a point where you will be disappointed but can resolve the minor distraction by asking for a napkin to wipe your stains away for instance. Do not leave when you had the original intentions to get some food but then left with none. That means you didn't accomplish your goal, and that can lead to feeling like you are going to have an unproductive day. You can carry around the burden and start to feel the wrong impact allowing it anger you or depress you when you come to grips with the shameful and embarrassing feel of it. At this point, we should leave it buried in the past so that it does not bother us when we are trying to accomplish our present goals. When you have to stand up before a crowd and speak before them. Ill feelings might grab a hold of you primarily because you are thinking how the crowd will perceive you to be. You are real nervous and tension actually builds up at this time because you not used to speaking before the crowd.

If mistakes are made, this can cause you to feel like walking away from the podium. The thing to do is relax your mood swing and stamina which will exude a period of restoration. Therefore, you do not come down hard on yourself. There also becomes a sign of relief as the burden has improved or been removed away from you as butterflies tend to ease. Ideally, you need to get over feeling of not allowing pent-up feelings to get the better of your emotions inside of you. It is best to be a confident person and stand up to your convictions.

A great suggestion is to be tough and strong when encountering a moment of feeling shamefulness. Take charge of responding to the accident/incident by realizing it was just an unfortunate situation at the time that it happened to transpire realizing mistakes can happen to anyone and no one is to blame. We take responsibility for our own actions and never mean to be disappointed at any situation, problem or circumstance. The truth of the matter is they just tend to creep up. It takes strong will power, tenacity and stamina to see that there is no reason for failure. You come out successful when you have moved to ease the burden thus, making you receive a unique, positive attitude towards accomplishing whatever the goal was in order to allow the feeling to subdue. Only then, will you overcome a feeling of being shameful, that is removing an emotional, intense desire to hold it down in your gut feelings. You don't always have to be a shameful person. You can overcome obstacles that are in the way and your fear of abandonment will cease causing you to accomplishing all your goals that you set out to achieve in life and you are not ashamed of achieving them.

CHAPTER 7
HOW TEDIOUS ARE YOU?

*T*edious generally means being bored in life. It is noted in the same category as a person having nothing better to do with themselves. We all find ourselves boring at different times in some situations but it is an active, good natured in spirit person though, that is never bored. When being shameful has taken a back seat, tedious specifies that a person has nothing better to strive for that may be exciting for the person experiencing boredom so he/she has not found an outlet to let out his or her desires and emotions get the better of themselves inside and out. You could say that it is a person is standing behind the scene and have not figured out a way to become involved actively in some fascinating past time in regards to reality. They want other people to have mercy on their soul.

They stay locked up inside and out sitting around feeling pity for themselves. If people are feeling this way, it is important to kind of break out of traditional patterns of behavior and take more of an exciting route. Being tedious is a lot like going to the same restaurant again and ordering the food and beverage, but your restaurant experiences aren't the same each time you go. Whether it's because a different cook makes your food or you have a different server, you feel like you continue to come here because it's convenient for you. Therefore, you are feeling a tedious mood swing because you lack change in your current situation. The same can be said, at an office job for example. The repeated nature of doing the same task often becomes tedious. If it's boring and not thrilling could put you at odds with feeling those negative vibrations which are not as important as moving towards a more positive solution away from feelings moments of being tedious in the same way, fashion, shape or form of doing the same type of job.

In most situations, tedious isn't because there is a lack of effort or dedication, but rather results in a loss of interest and/or excitement that would enhance one's ability to enjoy moments when a repeated nature is not occurring at this time. The overwhelming response is you will not be bored in whatever the circumstances may turn out to be because it is important not to stay caught in a rut. Thus, by knowing that you can break out of normal repeated routines and finding an outlet to channel your energies into something positive will improve the impact of a tedious, boring situation. Although tedious means that you are following traditional patterns of behavior, you must find a way to escape it. It is important to break free of moments of boredom and reach out for another alternative so a positive feeling will change your spirit of feeling those negative, false, implied and emotional responses to what was at first, a reaction that tended to often be misleading. Breaking out of a routine will make you get over being tedious as new outlets develop. For example, if having the same workout regimen is extremely tedious, when it's done correct and consistent, you will see amazing results. You can turn a tedious task around, and make yourself energetic, and master all the possibilities to stay in active frame of mind. In most situations, think before you act when in any tedious mood swing. Mentally, change your thinking habits and stick with the routine that best enable the feelings that are true in the heart. Continue to explore new doors of opportunity that will make you feel better in this process until a period of being a tedious, boring person has diminished away from you.

If you have felt a sudden loss of interest in some pastime, you should try your hand at something new. It is not advisable to tackle that project you have been delaying, never wanting to get the job done because it will only make you lose interest. There becomes a period of isolation to the point of asking yourself, will you continue to keep the same boring pace, or will you pick up speed and accomplish what you set out to do? Most people from time to time grow tired of the same, weary, repeated offensive behavior mood swing and want to find something else interesting to put their ideas, decisions and suggestions to work for them. It is after that, they are no longer feeling the down and out mood of tediousness but on a positive level, people will overcome a blank void in their present and/or future choices.

By going to someone you know to communicate and have interesting things to say when you are in dialogue with them lifts a heavy burden. The other person that you are talking to will want to listen to you and hear what you have to say. Perhaps, your conversation is interesting enough that the other person will not pass out nor will you put that other person to sleep. In a manner of speaking, "DO NOT BORE A PERSON WHEN YOU ARE TALKING TO THEM OTHERWISE, THEY MIGHT JUST WALK AWAY . . ."

We do not know how every implication of an encounter or invitation of circumstantial evidence will turn out to be. We only know we have be our p's and q's. We have the know-how to make something turn out interesting by putting it to the test. It is mind set plan that is plain as dwelling into something interesting when we are approached with an idea, plan or conception. It is strongly advisable to put away any uncertainty or misconception of wrongful doings, thoughts and suggestions. Only we as citizens will meet other people, talk out our differences and come up with solutions to close a generation gap in our society that tends to heal a wounded, broken heart that will turn out detrimental if we did not take care of it. A true known factor is that none of us want to be tedious individuals some of the time but we cannot help ourselves when we get stuck in a rut. The best thing for all of us to do is keep channeling our energies, drive and stamina into something realistic. It will release a period of annoyance about being extremely bored in some of life situations. Only then, will we know how to relax from this mood swing called, "tedious," escape from it, and no longer be a victim of it.

CHAPTER 8
WHAT DOES IT TAKE
TO BE SOCIABLE?

As life captures everyone's attention, what does it take to be sociable as citizens in our society? This is a question we can all answer because everywhere we go, people we encounter on our journeys and decisions we make every day being sociable is an aspect of it. If not, we might as citizens go through life feeling a period of isolation from the world in which we live in. A few, minor number of people choose though, to go through life living as a lonely person with nothing else to do or nobody to talk to. But, is there a way to defeat the purpose? Can you come out stronger on top as more of an individual socialite? Why, my belief is yes you can. You see when this happens; we are the type of people that always tend to get along with family members, friends and peers in society. We know how to handle something that impacts us socially.

First, there has to be a dedication and deep desire to stand up and speak out for what you believe in. Secondly, an effort to connect to other population genre is of vital importance when wanting to approach another individual and exchange one-on-one communication receiving positive feedback in the process. Third, there then becomes a will to succeed over any obstacles that precede standing before us. Fourth, you generally gather as much knowledge as possible when becoming sociable and come up with a final conclusion that best meets the needs of all parties concerned. These points are primarily due to social interactions. The more you strive to interact with others, the more of a sociable person we can all become. We are less condescending because interaction and communication are key vital points in socialization. There is a superior attitude in you as an individual and you stand out in all of your encounters in life. We are not worried individuals about failure, but only success when accomplishing our past, present and/or future goals.

It takes effort, dedication, and a will to succeed that makes you a person strong enough to approach the other individual. It is my belief that reaching out, you will witness that you both have something interesting to do or say. I always try and remember no matter how bad of a day, week, month and year that I have had, there is always somebody that has had it worse than myself. By being open and sharing issues breaks you out that social blockade because for one, you realize that there are other people with more unfortunate circumstances and the two of you are able to help each other. The more you can become sociable, the more you can have an impact on somebody's life because some people just need an ear to talk to you. Negative emotions will pour out of your chest like getting rid of a cold but the more times you treat it, it is not a disease you catch. It is how successful you can be as a communicator and being sociable is a mindset that no matter the adversity to your goals you will accomplish it, because the aftermath of the accomplished goal triumphs, and puts forth the work to achieve it. You are trustworthy and exude certain righteousness about you when you socialize with other people. With being sociable comes the ability to trust your instincts, no matter the rightfulness or wrongfulness of your conviction(s). You normally find yourself "stepping up" in occurrences when a character of socializing is necessary. Becoming sociable has a connection of caring for others also. You are generally a team player and will show leadership characteristics.

Good vibrations make you sociable by generally connecting to people that have some similarities like you. You normally go outside of your comfort zone to be in sociable situations so whenever you are in your most comfortable sociable times and areas, be openly sociable to whomever is willing to listen to you. Do not fear rejection when trying to become more sociable. Not everybody wants to be a listener to your problems and you can't necessarily force that among the public and vice-versa. Is it not everyone's fault that someone doesn't want to listen to your problems? It is a fine line, in order to gauge in but if we want to be sociable this will definitely make us become the aggressor. People always socialize once a dialect or dialogue has been opened up to start the communication process. Sometimes it takes other people to feel comfortable to open up and socialize even though they might be a more dominant personality type because comfort ability and communication are two key focal points that make you sociable. Therefore, you open up dialect and dialogue that is comfortable to you because you were the one who started the conversation in the first place. The response(s) you are getting back allows you to connect with other people socially and it is something that to an extent, every human being has encountered and had challenges with. It isn't something in regards to feeling like you are right or wrong, but forming lifelong connections with people, which never takes a break or has vacation time to do so with your connections. It is just that it happens naturally and so you connect with other people of population genre of various cultures.

Debra Fine's piece of literature entitled: *The Fine Art of Small Talk* states on page 37 in the chapter, *"Keep the Conversation Going" "Remember, instead of sitting back and waiting for another kind soul to start the conversation, take the lead. Think of it as if you invited that person to your home for dinner. As host, it's your job to see that your guest is comfortable. The same is true in conversation-try to make your guest feel as comfortable as possible. When you walk into a party or a gathering, find a person to meet. It's much easier to engage one person rather than enter a group conversation, so begin by looking for the "approachable person."*

If you do not feel that you are a sociable person generally means that in most social situations, you are the "negative Nancy" of the group. You are the "party pooper". You are the one trying to make the least out of a situation, social gathering or work problem, etc. and not adding any positive light into the encounter. If you are not a sociable type will lead to jealously, as you are trying to be pessimistic to take the negative and gloomiest point of view because you envy someone close to you that's optimistic. What you do to handle it is to see how you can increase your level of optimism not only for yourself. But, you know that you have the probability of bringing the socialite out of the both of you, while at the same time, there are no pessimistic feelings among you, another person or groups in question. Hoping for the best outcome is what you tend gain in being a sociable person when you are faced with pessimistic or optimistic people in society.

Both authors, *"Larry King with Bill Gilbert,"* writes in their piece of literature, *"How to Talk to Anyone, Anytime, Anywhere, The Secrets of Good Communication,"* and state on page 57, *"Don't Monopolize the Conversation."* *"A serious danger in social talk is to go on so long that you monopolize the conversation, turning yourself from a gifted conversationalist into a bore. Give those you talk to a chance to talk back-equal time, as we say in broadcasting. And, don't feel that you have to cross every t and dot every i by including every detail of a story you're telling. That's what people do after telling you, "To make a long story short . . ." When you hear that, get ready for a long story. Keep your own stories brief; the more people there are in your conversational group, the briefer they should be."*

A point in being sociable is getting to the heart of the conversation by being comprehensible thus, understanding truthful dialect which enhances one's ability to become the master of ceremony.

The act of grasping on to the basis of the nature of the conversation is important to understanding rhetoric as the art or study of using language effectively or persuasively so that you convince your audience. Verbal communication is a strong key focal point and never hurts anyone when a good conversationalist can talk up a great topic that is interesting.

A willingness to approach a person make a live, sociable person achieve successful relations with another person. There is nothing that stands in your way at this time because you are a strong person satisfying the status quo. All illusions, and skepticism subdue to the point of you indeed, not being of afraid of how to communicate past, present, and future accomplishments. But success or failure depends on how much you want to arrive at a point in your life where you can keep the communication seeking out both friendships and relationships where we must be sociable in society. In reality, it is a mood swing that we can surmount if we seriously consider what will be necessary to respond to open up and speak out about a matter we tend to become concerned about. When we are on our journeys and everyday walks of life and approached by someone in society, the question we might first ask ourselves is, "what does it take to be sociable?"

CHAPTER 9
HOW TO HANDLE
MOODINESS

$\mathcal{P}$eople in all walks of life have had issues since the beginning of time. These issues that transpire through our people in society feels like something called, "mood swings." As our society has adopted an attitude, of living a promising life that if we believe in something it will come to us naturally, we have been expecting to receive it in abundance. Do we always get what we want though, we expect the very best that life has to offer us, if we reach our goals. Times can be hard for some people and easier for others. The real truth in the matter is that not all people are viewed in the same category so some may receive it more than others. Consequently, when a person finds themselves trying to act like another person, may cause for some disappointment because you may be trying to be something that you are not totally alike. Can they achieve status because every person has differences of opinion in communicating thoughts, feelings and desires? It's no surprise that all this emotional intensity can have a serious impact on your feelings but there are easier and natural ways to keep your spirits lifted up. Be careful though, you should not want to lose touch with reality and living a life in the end that is not pleasing to you. Intellectual faculties caused by the mind's power at any time tend to invade a person's way of adjusting to society morally. They have a tremendous impact on your life mentally, physically and socially and emotionally. We realize that only we as people react to different stigma that occurs but there are decisions that we must face allowing us to know our real self from where we know the end result will turn out to actually be.

Both positive and negative reinforcement causes a mood swing to be perceived as an attraction to the senses. This will cause people to experience any temperament of a mood that would make a person's life stand out a certain way as the mood takes place in the individual. It increases a likelihood that a given response will recur in a situation like that in which the reinforcing condition originally occurred. What happens at this point is that it is each human being's reaction to it will make us interact differently with one another as we all grow up in an environment where our lives are viewed individually. Do not panic! Enjoy the mood swing transpiring at the time by handling it in a positive manner. Move to resolve a negative impact of a situation/circumstance that can take its toll on you. For example, a feeling such as if you have been made to feel less superior around your contacts or being wronged in society. Real issues in life has a major impact on us to be able to deal with any type of mood swing as it transpires. The reality of it is we all act differently as a person based on our behavior, attitude and characteristics when we born into this world. It is going to make us relate to ourselves either positively or negatively based on how we are all perceived to be different people growing up in this society. We cannot change this but we can make a difference by acting responsibly according to our beliefs.

We are a people of many races, color, gender, sexes, and creed. We must consider that all people have different traits, genes and behavioral characteristics. Our personal genetic makeup means that we do not have the same type of skin tone, eyes are pictured very differently, and our bodies are not all shaped the same. Our dimensions have an extremely serious impact on our mood swings we encounter daily from when we wake up in the morning until we go to sleep at night because we would not see the world through a microscopic lens. The mood swing will enter into a person's life and set the pace for an individual to adopt an attitude that would make us feel emotions from our sensory perception of perceiving things done differently. When we look at a person who is generally high-spirited, they do not allow someone to bring their world down, for instance. They always rise above the occasion putting any negativity on themselves out of them to feel generally feel good about themselves again. You do not classify them with a person who is feeling negative vibes on the other hand, and may feel that they will be down casted by something or someone in society. The impact is so strong on the individual mind though; that there is a reaction which allows their feelings to rule over their life beyond their control no matter what their internal and external circumstances turn out to be. It is easier to deal with a mood swing when you are aware of your capabilities. You should use feelings from a talent or ability that has the potential for development or use of something transpiring for successful outcomes. People have various ups and downs, and high and low moments in life that impact them as a person. If they do not search for a better outcome, then people may experience problems not caused by one's own self but have developed for no particular reason. Simply put, the stronger person will expect though, positive resolutions that does not allow a problem to fester in own life for enormous periods of time thus, knowing the encounter will turn out a success story.

It is certain that we should be responsible for our own actions by taking charge of our mood swings we encounter daily. Then, people take control of their own lives after experiencing episodes of happiness, grief, anxiety or by being a socialite with other people. One of the things to do is find someone to help you through the mood swing if there are problems dealing with it. If we seek guidance know that it will be offered to you. We should always know that you have help somewhere. The internet *(wikihow.com)* says do these simple steps: (1) **Take Deep Breathes.** Try to relax. This will clear your head. (2) **Write down how you're feeling and why you think you might be feeling this way.** It could lead you to the source of the problem. (3) **Pinch yourself.** While it might not be the most comfortable thing in the world, it will snap you out of your hectic mood. (4) **Move around.** Clench and unclench your fists, bounce your legs up and down, or just take a walk. Anything that involves your being active. And, (5) **Keep in mind that every day is a blessing.** Lay down and think positive thoughts. By doing this, it will mirror or reflect how to handle different moods based on real issues in life perceived by yourself and people whom you have an encounter with. Mood swings happen to everyone. If you are overcome by anger for instance, and brought back to tears, this could lead to a feeling of being completely hopeless and out of focus. You must go directly to the source and confront it. Your pastor, family and friends can all be of help. You will be able to make proper decisions on how life can improve for you. Remember, the longer you take to cure your problem the more difficult it becomes to conquer it. Do not be afraid of failure, as it only allows you to analyze your mistakes. Stay positive, and make good/knowledgeable decisions. The attitude, challenge and effect of the mood swing will work out far better than you would have imagined once you have reached a responsible means to achieving your goal. You will gain a new perspective on life that resolves any circumstantial evidence and allows the mood swing to take its course in many leaps and boundaries.

It is important to always be self-accountable for your actions, and if you didn't do anything wrong do not blame yourself. That creates self-doubt, which can lead to one of the many negative mood swings discussed. It is important to be open-minded and stay positive even though sometimes you are going to feel like you need to vent off frustration. Always communicate any problem that you feel like is bigger than what you can handle. Remember approaching the problem head on is major stepping stone to achieving results. By doing this, you may have had a mood swing transpire and based on what kind it was, either you enjoyed it or overcame the real issue in life to achieve momentum and success.

EPILOGUE . . .

"This piece of literature was developed after an ideology to share information about why there are human intellectual faculties in the power of the mind which makes a certain stigmatism happen to develop systematically. As some people in our society have an enormous desire to offer some consultation to people of all kinds that encounter various mood swings when facing an uplifting or life threatening situation, you would never expect it to happen on its own so the reality shocks people. They do become aware that it is a mood swing that will transpire at any given time, hypothetically speaking. Most people choose to deal with the real issue that tends to invade a person's lifestyle no matter whether the implication is a positive or negative development. The details in this piece of literature explain how we as people could become impacted when we respond to real issues based on what makes a person experience a typical mood swing in our population genre. By opening up and facing the real issue in life in general, is why it is important for us as individuals to successfully overcome a generation gap in our society."

Bibliography . . .

Shimoff, Marci. *Happy For No Reason, 7 Steps To Being Happy From The Inside Out.* New York, NY: Free Press, 2008. Print.

Spencer, Amy. *Bright Side Up, 100 Ways to Be Happier Right Now.* New York, NY: Penguin Group, 2012. Print.

Van Praagh, James. *Healing Grief, Reclaiming Life After Any Loss.* New York, NY: Penguin Group, 2000. Print.

Cornils, Stanley P. *The Mourning After, How to Manage Grief Wisely.* Saratoga, CA: R&E Publishers, 1990. Print.

Burns, M.D., David D. *Feeling Good, The New Mood Therapy.* New York, NY: Harper Collins Publisher, Inc., 1980. Print.

MacFarlaine, Muriel, R.N., M.A.. *The Panic Attack, Phobia Solutions Handbook.* Encinitas, CA: United Research Publishers, 1996. Print.

Emmons, Henry, M.D.. *The Chemistry Of Calm, Settle Your Mind, Reclaim Healthy Emotions, Stop Worrying, And Start Fully Living.* New York, NY: Touchstone Simon Schuster, Inc., 2010. Print.

Smith, Ian K., M.D.. *Happy, Simple Steps To Get The Most Out Of Life.* New York, NY: United States of America, 2010. Print.

Fine, Debra. *The Fine Art Of Small Talk, How To Start A Conversation, Keep It Going, Build Networking Skills And Leave A Positive Impression.* New York, NY: Hyperion Harper Collins, 2005. Print.

King, Larry, Bill Gilbert. *How To Talk To Anyone, Anytime, Anywhere, The Secrets Of Good Communication.* New York, NY: Crown Publishers, Inc., 1994. Print.

INTERNET

(Domains)

http://www.moods.com
http://www.happiness.com
http://www.anxiety.com
http://www.depression.com
http://www.excitement.com
http://www.wikipedia.com
http://www.ehow.com
http://www.ask.com